STURDY TURTLES

by Kathleen Martin-James

Lerner Publications Company • Minneapolis

Website address: www.lernerbooks.com

Curriculum Development Director: Nancy M. Campbell

Words in *italic type* are explained in a glossary on page 30.

Library of Congress Cataloging-in-Publication Data

Martin-James, Kathleen
    Sturdy turtles / by .Kathleen Martin-James.
        p.   cm. — (Pull ahead books)
    Includes index.
    Summary: Introduces the physical characteristics, behavior, and habitat of North American turtles.
    ISBN 0-8225-3627-7 (hc. : alk. paper). —
    ISBN 0-8225-3631-5 (pbk. : alk. paper)
    1. Turtles—Juvenile literature.
[1. Turtles.] I. Title. II. Series.
QL666.C5M28 2000
597.92—dc21   99–11364

Manufactured in the United States of America
1 2 3 4 5 6 – JR – 05 04 03 02 01 00

Look carefully! What is peeping
at you from inside this shell?

This animal is a turtle.
All turtles have shells.

Turtle shells are made of bone.
They are strong and sturdy.

The top of a shell is the *carapace*.
The bottom is the *plastron.*

A turtle cannot leave its shell.
Its shell is part of its body.

A shell helps keep a turtle safe from *predators.*

Predators are animals that hunt and eat other animals.

A turtle can pull its head, legs, and tail inside its shell to hide.

If a predator flips a turtle over,

the turtle uses its head and
neck to turn right side up.

Turtles come in many shapes
and colors.

This turtle is called a spotted
turtle. Do you know why?

Some turtles have soft shells. This turtle is called a smooth softshell.

It lives in water.
It has *webbed feet.*

Animals with webbed feet
have skin joining their toes.

This skin helps them paddle
in the water and swim quickly.

All turtles have *scales* growing out of their skin.

Scales are like fingernails. They are hard and strong.

Open wide! Like all turtles,
this snapping turtle has no teeth.

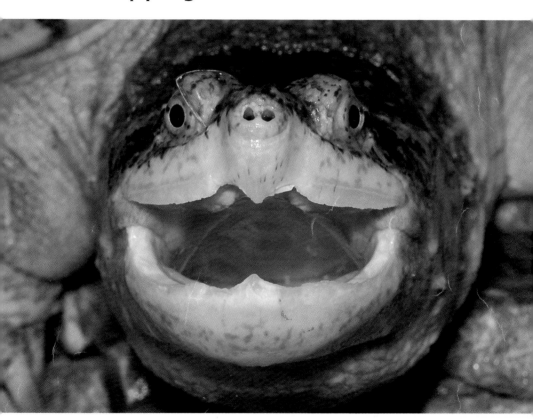

How can a toothless turtle eat?

It uses its *beak* to rip up its food.

A beak is a hard mouth
with sharp edges.

Turtles eat plants and small animals like worms. Turtles are *omnivores.*

Omnivores are animals that eat both plants and animals.

This turtle is sitting in the shade to
cool off. How do turtles warm up?

Turtles sit in the sun to warm up.

A turtle is a kind of animal called an *ectotherm.*

An ectotherm's body heat changes to match the heat or cold around it.

Because turtles are
ectotherms with scales,

they belong to a group
of animals called *reptiles.*

Like most reptiles, turtles have babies that come from eggs.

This mother turtle is digging a hole in the dirt for her eggs.

She lays
many soft
eggs in the
hole.

The turtle covers her eggs
with dirt to hide them.

Then she leaves them.

If a predator like a raccoon
finds the eggs, it will eat them.

What
happens
if the eggs
stay hidden?

Surprise! Baby turtles *hatch* from the eggs in a few months.

Baby turtles
are tiny.
Their shells
are soft.

As a turtle grows,
its shell becomes stronger.

Soon it will be a sturdy turtle.

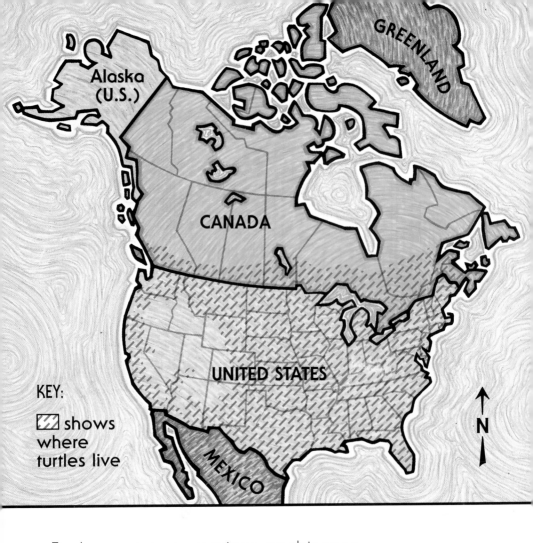

KEY:

⬚ shows where turtles live

Find your state or province on this map.
Do turtles live near you?

Parts of a Turtle's Body

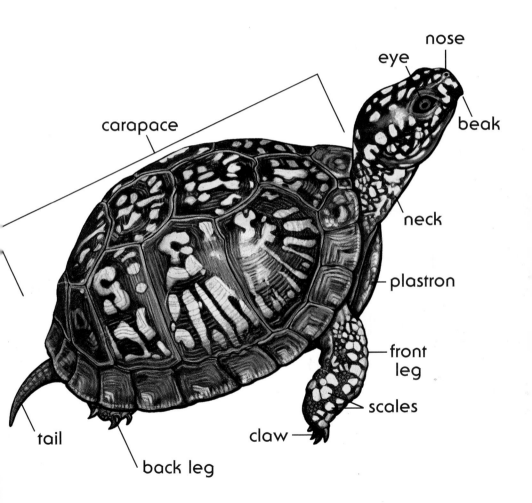

nose

eye

carapace

beak

neck

plastron

front
leg

scales

tail

claw

back leg

Glossary

beak: a hard mouth with sharp edges

carapace: the top part of a turtle shell

ectotherm: an animal whose body heat changes to match the heat or cold around it

hatch: come out

omnivores: animals that eat both plants and animals

plastron: the bottom part of a turtle shell

predators: animals that hunt and eat other animals

reptiles: crawling or creeping animals that usually have scales. A reptile's body heat changes to match the heat or cold around it. (Snakes, alligators, lizards, and turtles are reptiles.)

scales: a reptile's strong, hard skin covering

webbed feet: feet that have skin joining the toes

Hunt and Find

The publisher wishes to extend special thanks to our **series consultant,** Sharyn Fenwick. An elementary science-math specialist, Mrs. Fenwick was the recipient of the National Science Teachers Association 1991 Distinguished Teaching Award. In 1992, representing the state of Minnesota at the elementary level, she received the Presidential Award for Excellence in Math and Science Teaching.

About the Author

Mike Dembeck

Kathleen Martin-James was born in Toronto, Ontario. She has lived in many different places across Canada and in the United States. She began spending a lot of time with turtles when she met her husband, Mike, who is a turtle biologist. Kathleen writes articles and takes photographs for magazines, newspapers, and newsletters. She loves to read and to write stories and poems. Kathleen lives in Wolfville, Nova Scotia, with Mike and their turtles, Scout (shown above) and Felix.

Photo Acknowledgments

The photographs in this book are reproduced through the courtesy of: © Bill Beatty/Visuals Unlimited, pages 3, 8; © Dale Jackson/Visuals Unlimited, page 24; © Joe McDonald/Visuals Unlimited, pages 4, 21; © Dan Nedrelo, front and back covers, pages 6, 7, 9, 14, 15, 16, 18, 22, 26, 27; © Patrice/Visuals Unlimited, page 11; © David T. Roberts/Nature's Images Inc., page 23; © Kjell B. Sandved/Visuals Unlimited, page 25; © David M. Schleser/Nature's Images Inc., page 13; © A. B. Sheldon, pages 10, 17, 19, 20, 31; © Rob and Ann Simpson/Visuals Unlimited, page 5; © Gustav W. Verderber/Visuals Unlimited, page 12.